PRAYERS FOR THE PREY

The Escape Plan to Overcoming Sexual Abuse

ERICA T CAPRI

Gemlight Publishing LLC

Gulfport, Mississippi

Prayers for the Prey

Copyright © 2020 Gemlight Publishing LLC

Gulfport, MS 39507

All Rights Reserved

ISBN: 9781734432640

Unless otherwise stated, all scriptures and citation is from the Holy Bible, NIV, Copyright ©1973, 1978 by International Bible Society. All rights reserved. Printed in the United States of America.

No part of this publication may be reproduced, stored in a retrieval system, or transmitted, in any form or by any means electronic, mechanical, photocopying, recording, or otherwise, without the prior written permission of the author, except in the case of brief quotations embodied in critical articles and reviews.

Cover by: Gemlight Publishing Designs

Illustrations by Freepix.com

Printed in the United States of America

TABLE OF CONTENTS

Author's Note	6
Acknowledgement	8
Introduction	9

1. Finding The Key to VALUE — 13
   - Why Me? — 14
   - Moving On — 18
   - Baby You're Worth It — 22

2. Unlocking the door to you VISION — 26
   - Who Am I? — 27
   - Waiting — 30
   - Boldly Exposed — 33

3. Walk into the door of VICTORY — 36
   - Hit me with your best shot — 37
   - Building Power — 40
   - The Beginning of Winning — 43

4. Prayer for the Prey Poem — 47
5. Putting Prayer to Action Exercises — 50
6. About the Author — 60

AUTHOR'S NOTE

If you're reading this, it delights me to know that you've chosen to step outside your comfort zone to learn, understand, and outgrow your pain. Indeed, there is an escape plan from being the prey (victim) to becoming a predator, to crawl victoriously out of that dark path and never to travel there again.

As women, our kindness and vulnerability has been taken advantage of, our decision to "Keep Silent" has been ridiculed and perceived as weakness by the enemy, and our bodies, minds, and souls have been stolen and held hostage for far too long. To the world, we have lost our value, vision, and victory to the beast of abuse, but to our maker, we are whole and strong. As we wait in silence, the enemy moves, but our maker beckons persistently "rise up and take charge, my child". Now, our patience have been stretched thin. It's time to take back what the enemy has stolen!

You will no longer be defined by the world but by yourself. You will find yourself in God's word and proclaim it loudly from the mountain top. It's time to level up and live the abundant life that God promised, a life of peace and prosperity.

As you commit yourself to these prayers, my desire is that your daily participation will draw you closer to your maker, God, who loves you earnestly and has great plans for you. I also pray that your inner beauty be unveiled and the greatness inside you that's yearning for expression be audaciously unleashed. May every word and prayer that is spoken by you, challenge your inner self and make you ANEW!

God Bless,

Erica T Capri

Acknowledgement

I thank God, who is the redeemer of my soul; without him, my life would've not been possible.

To my dear friend, John, who inspired me to share my story with women who have walked the same dark past as me. Because of him, I overcame domestic abuse, mental illness, depression, and self-esteem issues. With him and God, this has empowered me to be the successful woman I am today.

Also, to my mother, who is my number one fan in all of my writing endeavors!

INTRODUCTION

The first step to healing and taking charge is self-reflection. Reflect on these questions and dig deep within;

> Do you remember when and what life felt like before you were attacked?

> How did it feel to suddenly become helpless or unable to defend yourself when it first happened?

> What did it feel like to come out and pretend as though nothing had happened, while suffering immensely on the inside?

> How many times have you endured similar attacks over the course of time?

What impact has it had on your lifestyle, sexual preferences, and/or mental wellbeing? As a result, are you nymphomania, a bisexual, a femme, or mentally ill?

How does the world see, define, or label you or the secret that's hidden within you that no one sees nor understands how you feel? Take a deep breath, my dearest Queen, you are not alone. In 2 Samuel 13:1-22, the beautiful daughter of King David, named Tamar, experienced what you've endured. The violation, especially of someone close to you, can damage your heart. Tamar was molested by her half-brother, Amnon. When Tamar reached puberty, her half-brother David's eldest son, developed an unnatural obsession with her. Being young and naïve, she was tricked into sexual immorality. As the result, she met a traumatizing fate, which made her unworthy of marriage, having lost her virginity. So, you see? With God, there is nothing new under the sun and there's always justice and restoration. But, why you? I get it. It's not fair that you were the prey, caught in the middle of the predator's hunt. Like you, I too have wondered, "where and when did the practice of abuse start and what could make a man think that it's okay to prey on a woman's innocence?" The answer is right before us. It's a generational shift, which started when our ancestors were in bondage. Young women were forced to marry

older men, and they were expected to do nothing but cook, clean, have sex, and bear children. And even though times and laws have changed, the mindsets of certain people haven't.

No, it not fair that you had to be the victim of a savage mindset that has trapped so many men, who somehow deem it appropriate to take advantage of innocent little girls and young vulnerable ladies. Many women battle daily to wash away their devastation of sexual abuse by shedding endless tears, just like Tamar from the bible. But, this is a spirit that has, and is still dwelling on this earth. So, it is up to us, the women who suffered this pain, to prevent our daughters, granddaughters, nieces, sisters, and cousins from entering the earthly pit of Hell (a lonely hole of condemnation, where you lose sight of yourself and your worth). Trust me, I know the feeling. The one where you're disconnected from your body and the endless struggle of recognizing your self-worth and respect. However, trying to find joy, both on the inside and out, can be challenging without a strong prayer life. Thankfully, every traumatizing event can be healed, but only by God. What you suffered is now in the past – the deed is done! Don't let the loneliness and shame you endured to be in vain.

Thus, in keeping with His word, my friend, I have written this book – a strategic plan for helping you escape devastating mind wars and come out with the swords of VALUE, VISION, & VICTORY. With these swords, everything you were powerless to overcome will become easily surmountable.

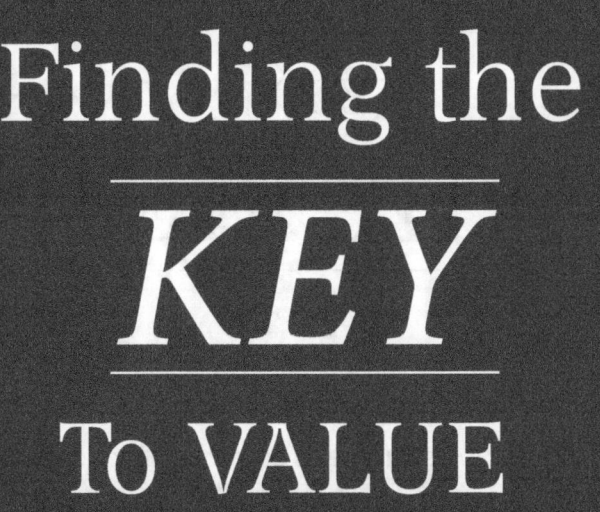

Finding the KEY To VALUE

Value; worth, utility, or importance

"

Know your worth, then add the tax

WHY ME?

Feeling fatal worthlessness. Have you ever wondered why you struggle to command the respect of others? If so, those moments stem from your self-loathing and feelings of undervalue and worthlessness.

Often, when we have been criminally violated, without brutal force or guns, and forced to keep silent, we question ourselves – "WHY ME?" Our life births the feelings of insecurity and soon after, we conclude that there must be something wrong with us to have been touched in the wrong way, assaulted, or violated.

Over time, that negative feeling grows and ripens to total numbness, and then, we begin hurting others who love us. We can, sometimes, convert the burden of hate for our predators to doubts and self-hatred.

But, here's why you should expel negativity from your thoughts – God has set you on a wonderful path to a great destiny, then comes the enemy to steal, kill, and destroy. You'd be mistaken to think that predator-prey situations are a matter of strength and weakness. No! The enemy has one goal and one mission – to

snatch away the destiny God has called you to fulfill – and he'll do that by any means necessary. In the end, just like the walls of Jericho, you must pull down your masks and stand naked – in spirit – before the world.

With brevity and a wide smile to spite the enemy, say out loud; "WHY NOT ME? I'm extraordinary. If I wasn't a rare gem, the enemy wouldn't find me worthy enough to attack and attempt to destroy. I'm a threat to the enemy! I know that now! So, yes! I may have suffered an Incest, but I survived. Yes! I was raped, but I still have even some of my sanity. Yes! My innocence was taken, but my life and purpose was unscathed. I'm too hard of a nut for the enemy to crack. I have been given this 'optional' rich LIFE and so great a destiny. I choose to live. God is my Captain and I am the passenger.

What God Says

1 Corinthians 6:20

"For God bought you with a high price. So, you must honor God with your body."

Matthew 6:26

"Look at the birds. They don't plant or harvest or store food in barns, for your heavenly Father feeds them. And aren't you far more valuable to him than they are?"

Jeremiah 29:11

"For I know the plans I have for you, declares the Lord, plans for welfare and not for evil, to give you a future and a hope."

Isaiah 49:16

"Behold, I have graven thee upon the palms of my hands; thy walls are continually before me."

Express yourself * notes*

_____
_____
_____
_____

Your daily affirmation!

"A beautiful thing is never perfect"

Prayer

Lord, grant me the knowledge and the strength to accept the hurdles that has been predestined according to your divine destiny for my life.

Give me strength when I am weak, courage to continue this journey, a forgiveness heart to accommodate those who have hurt me, and the boldness to know my worth and value.

Help me to feel your presence when you are near and at all times.

This, I pray in your son, Jesus' name,

Amen.

MOVING ON

Letting go is the hard part that requires hard work. Getting over the traumas of a baggage-filled past is tough and can take some time. However, forgiveness (of self) sets the foundation on new grounds for moving on – you can't start a new chapter in your life while re-living the same old one. that , where as, Failure to overcome the feelings of guilt and hurt is not only the biggest mistake you can make but the greatest repressor of your growth.

Guilt plants the seed of disvalue. Once planted, the seed is watered by the feelings of insecurity. When cultured together, you'll begin convincing yourself that you're not good enough, pretty enough, or strong enough to protect yourself. Every time you question your abilities or inabilities, you're essentially watering the seed of pain. As it matures into an entrapping stronghold of hurt, your heart becomes a battlefield for anyone that comes close.

It takes the power of healing to move on from disadvantage and pain, and to let go of what has been

stolen or hijacked from you. To heal, you must lay down all the pain at Jesus feet and allow God to mend your heart. Satan seeks to keep you focused on what has you bound, but the secret to moving on is forgiving yourself.

Go look in the mirror right away and tell me what you see. Do you see a beautiful strong woman who believes in herself, knowing that a lost diamond is another King's precious jewel? Do you believe in yourself? Do you believe your future is filled with abundant joy and love? Don't let sexual abuse deceive you that life is purposeless. Don't let your past control your mental health and leave you depressed. Stop neglecting self-care because you don't feel beautiful enough. Pick yourself up, polish your mind, move on, and embrace your future. Be the light and shine unabashedly.

You want a change, I know it and I can feel it. That's why you picked up this book. So, forget your past – the hurt, pain, love, and trials. Overcome all of it with the power that God has given you. I believe that this is your season for self-discovery and unconditional love.

What God Says

Philippians 3:13
"Brothers, I do not consider that I have made it my own. But one thing I do: forgetting what lies behind and straining forward to what lies ahead."

Isaiah 43:18
"Forget what happened in the past, and do not dwell on events from long ago".

Romans 8:5
"For they that are after the flesh do mind the things of the flesh; but they that are after the Spirit, the things of the Spirit."

Express yourself * notes*

_____
_____
_____
_____
_____

Your daily affirmation!
"Life is like riding a bicycle, to keep your balance, you must keep moving." — Albert Einstein

Prayer

Lord, please forgive me for all the sins I have committed. It's hard for me to see past my pain, so I ask that you give me the 20/20 vision to the destiny you have in-store for me. Where I am weak, please make me strong so that I don't settle for less than what I deserve. I need your help and guidance to move forward with peace of mind.

This, I pray in your son, Jesus' name,

Amen.

BABY, YOU'RE WORTH IT!

Knowing our value, changes our faith. When I am at my worst, I, sometimes, doubt my true value, but I never let it affect my outward appearance. Anytime I look into the mirror, regardless of whether or not I see God's image, I try never to allow my emotions to control my attitude. Instead, I begin to speak into existence, the image that God created me to be.

I'm sure you agree that, sometimes, we can be too hard on ourselves for no good reason. So, whenever I'm about to give myself a hard time, I remember the scripture, "Created to do good works which God prepared in advance for us to do." (Eph. 2:10) and "Blessed is she who has believed that the Lord would fulfill his promises to her!"(Lu. 1:45).

In our society, predators always hunt for prey and women are more likely to be victims of acts of wickedness and injustice. But, we must grow past the "damaged goods" and "voiceless victim" labels and

own our true identity as women who are worth it. We cannot erase our past, but we can take control of our future.

When you value yourself at a bargain, then, expect whatever coin is tossed at your feet. But, if you would embrace your royal identity, as a queen, then, know that you were made to adorn palaces. You are priceless and too valuable to have your heart displayed for free or at a discount. As a queen, you are worth more than you know.

In the book of Esther 1:11, Queen Vashti was told to appear "wearing only her royal crown," according to the rabbinical tradition during her time—in other words, she was told to appear naked. Queen Vashti refused because she did not want to be put on display at a feast, providing entertainment before a group of salacious, drunken men. Although her decision caused humiliation to the King and was at the expense of her royal position, she knew and embraced the consequences of refusing the king.

Vashti may not have been recognized as a biblical role model (because of God's plans for Esther and the Jews), but she discovered her true value. Can you do the same? Can you stand your ground and stop settling for less? Even Esther wouldn't have appeared naked for the King's amusement.

Of course, you can find your own voice and your own value. Yes! As women, we were born to WIN!

What God Says

Jeremiah 31:3

"Yes, I have loved you with an everlasting love; therefore, with lovingkindness I have drawn you"

Romans 5:8

"But God demonstrates His own love toward us, in that while we were still sinners, Christ died for us."

Express yourself * notes*

_____
_____
_____
_____

Your daily affirmation!

"It is confidence in our bodies, minds, and spirits that allows us to keep looking for new adventures."— Oprah Winfrey

Prayer

Lord, it's me again. I feel a lot better understanding more about my true value, But, I still need more guidance to fully overcome my past.

Can you continue to strengthen my heart and soul to push through with the vision you have for me?

This, I pray in your son, Jesus' name.

Amen.

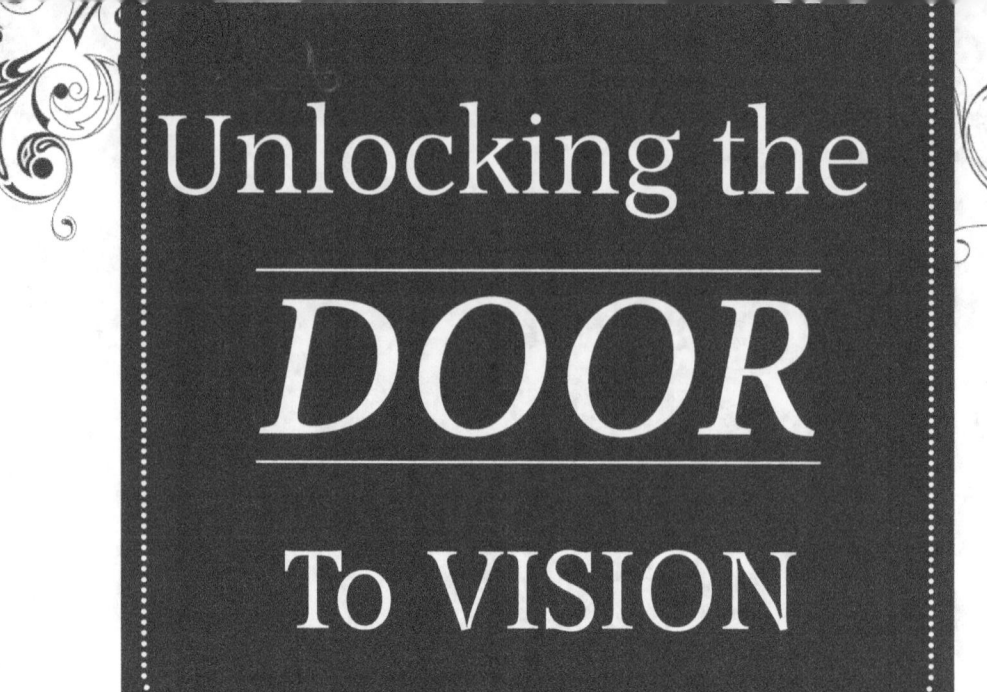

Vision; a picture of your future, as in a dream or a goal.

Dissatisfaction and discouragement are not caused by the absence of things but the absence of vision."

WHO AM I?

Life can make or break your goals. To achieve your vision and fulfill your dreams in life, you must know who you really are in Christ. You must find your identity before you can share your life with friends or a soul mate.

Often, we accept the identity we've been given by others. Identities like; "Bitter Woman" who lacks joy and self-pride. For example, in the bible (Lev.15:25), a woman who suffered prolonged menstruation for 12 years, was labelled 'unclean' by the public. She was also disqualified from marriage, which caused her immense trauma since she wasn't given an opportunity to live a normal life. But in Luke 8:43-48, we see how the woman with the an condition refused to be held back by society, fought for years and although all of her efforts were futile, she made a choice to keep trying, and she was determined in her heart that when she saw an opportunity, she would take it – it was her dream! So, when an opportunity presented itself, she made the tough call – to reach out and touch Jesus to receive her healing. She took a big risk in order to realize her vision.

Just like this woman, you must see yourself as a jewel that God has placed on this earth with a purpose, and not just to suffer or endure endless pain. Trusting God to help you discover your vision sound great, right? Turning it all to Him and letting Him be your GPS through life's ups and downs will ensure you shall overcome. There is no way to underestimate what God will and can do in your life, you only have to believe in his vision for you.

What God Says

Proverbs 3:5-6

"Trust in the LORD with all your heart, and lean not on your own understanding; in all your ways acknowledge Him, and He shall direct your paths."

Proverbs 29:18

"Where there is no vision, the people are unrestrained, But happy is he who keeps the law"

Express yourself * notes*

_____

_____

_____

Your daily affirmation!

"Failed plans should not be interpreted as a failed vision. Visions don't change, they are only refined. Plans rarely stay the same, and are scrapped or adjusted as needed. Be stubborn about the vision, but flexible with your plan".—John C Maxwell

Prayer

Lord, I need you to show me every good and perfect gift from above – coming down from the Father of the Heavens. Lead me, in Your righteousness from the enemies of my past. Shield me with your favor and protection from the tongue of deceit and malice. Please let the word of my heart be acceptable to you in this season.

This, I pray in your son, Jesus' name,

Amen.

WAITING

Impatience results in poor judgment. Being patience is a natural attribute of a woman, especially when she has attained motherhood status. However, when it comes to wanting something, patience becomes her greatest enemy, because, instead of following God's guidance, we want to rush God ,which leads to disappointments.

As the weaker vessels, we are more vulnerable, so we must not adopt a microwave mindset as we go through life. We may want our lives to be quick and easy, but we must understand that God has the red light on for a reason. It's a lot more practical to think about it this way since patience is a steep virtue.

If you've jumped quickly into a relationship and it doesn't work out, you must wait because God is transitioning you to a place that is voided of distractions. He wants you to discover yourself, love yourself, cater to yourself, and forgive yourself so you can be open and more prepared to fulfill your destiny.

When you don't wait to hear the voice of God, you may find yourself on the dark road back to repeating

your past mistakes, and as a result of your unwise and impatient judgments.

When the green light comes on, you will know, but until then, you will have to understand that patience is a valuable asset to your vision in life.

What God Says

> Galatians 6:9
>
> "Let us not become weary in doing good, for at the proper time we will reap a harvest if we do not give up."

> Romans 12:12
>
> "Be joyful in hope, patient in affliction, faithful in prayer."

 Express yourself * notes*

_____
_____
_____
_____
_____

Your daily affirmation!

"Patience is passion tamed." — Lyman Abbott

Prayer

Lord, I thank you for continuing to lead me to a better place. Please forgive me for my sinful nature. Just like the fruits of the spirit, I want more joy, love, peace, kindness, goodness, faithfulness, gentleness, self-control, and most of all, patience.

My spirit is yearning for more and more.

I'm sick of the weary nights, I'm sick of harboring hatred toward people.

Help me to be more like you, and to wait patiently for the good work you are doing in and through me.

This, I pray in your son, Jesus' name,

Amen.

BOLDLY EXPOSED

A desperate soul becomes slanderous. You'd be surprised how many women feel desperately lonely but are in denial. We live in a society, where women are more desperate for expression than men. However, when you're desperate, you make mistakes, poor choices, and atrocious life decisions.

Yes, it may have been difficult to stay silent for many years – protecting the wicked predator who severely attacked you. However, you must decide to be different from your predator. You must not let your experience influence your demeanor. Let your past experience motivate you to practice nobility.

Nothing is hidden under the sun, similarly, there'll come a time for our experiences in life to gain exposure for our healing. But before, during, or after your healing process, you must be at peace with yourself. And, as you decide to 'spill the beans', you must learn how to do so in humility, not anger and resentment.

It takes boldness to address sensitive matters with maturity.

What God Says

Psalm 138:3

"On the day I called, You answered me; You made me bold with strength in my soul."

2 Corinthians 4:8-10

"We are afflicted in every way, but not crushed; perplexed, but not driven to despair; persecuted, but not forsaken; struck down, but not destroyed; always carrying in the body the death of Jesus, so that the life of Jesus may also be manifested in our bodies."

✎ Express yourself * notes*

_____
_____
_____
_____
_____

Your daily affirmation!

"True humility is having the understanding that, even as a small seed, we are still an important part of the greater plan. However, we are not the master planner".
— Tanya Copprue

Prayer

Lord, I meditate on all your works and mighty deeds. I need your power to keep me humble in your eyes and in the eyes of your people. This has been the tough part for me, but I know that you will not put more on me than I can bear. My arms are stretched wide open, waiting for you to continue to comfort me during this journey.

This, I pray in your son, Jesus' name,

Amen.

Walk into the _DOOR_ of VICTORY

Victory; (1) the overcoming of an enemy or antagonist, (2) the achievement of mastery or success in a struggle or endeavor against odds or difficulties.

"Victory is sweeter once we taste defeat."

HIT ME WITH YOUR BEST SHOT

A steady progress is the strongest punch.

You are now the leading lady in your own war and so far, you are winning – you have grown a closer relationship with God and you now understand the queer motives of the wicked and the low level of your enemy. Girl, you are now a Boss-Lady, balling with victory by your side.

Was it easy getting to this point in your life? No! The price of Victory is quality time. You must take time to analyze your enemy to predict their next approach. You can't get to the winning stage in life if you remain in denial and avoid the healing process.

As victorious women, we can no longer sweat the small things that are foolish but understand God's will in everything. We will no more drown our problems in alcohol or numb our pain with sex and drugs. Instead, we choose to be above and bigger than the enemy. We choose to be filled with the spirit of Victory that enables us to overcome our giants.

Have you ever been consistent with a good habit and your progress made you feel good? Hang on to that for as long as God gives grace. You are now writing a new diary of your destiny and walking with victory into your future.

What God Says

> **Romans 8:38-39**
>
> "For I am sure that neither death nor life, nor angels nor rulers, nor things present nor things to come, nor powers, nor height nor depth, nor anything else in all creation, will be able to separate us from.

✎ Express yourself * notes*

_____
_____
_____
_____

Your daily affirmation!

"The first place we must win the victory is in our own minds. If you don't think you can be successful, then you never will be." — Joel Osteen

Prayer

Lord, clothe me with a victorious garment in every war against my enemies. Help me to tame my talk and walk with you. As I get rid of all forms of bitterness, rage, anger, or malice, shield me with redemption.

Forgive me, O God, and as I move on in victory, strengthen my heart to know that I am not on my own. Please be the leader in my ongoing battles.

This, I pray in your son, Jesus' name,

Amen.

BUILDING POWER

Your power must be secured. Every time you share your story with someone who is broken, every time you open up your heart, every time you walk in forgiveness, you prove that you have outgrown your past and have gained more muscle and the power to be over your circumstance. You've had a godly influence on that friend, co-worker, neighbor, or stranger.

It's a great feeling to boldly wield this power that comes only from God. It took a lot of uplifting, commitment, and forgiveness to overlook that pain and to claim your crown of power. You must guard this power and must not take it lightly. The enemy is always armed to exert wickedness. Predators are thirsty, hungry, and ready to prey on God's chosen. Therefore, you must be ready for every battle that comes your way. Put on your full armor and take a firm stand against the devil's schemes – the armor of power.

Your ....

P- Powerful,

O- Overcomer,

W- Worthy,

E- Empowered and

R- Royal

With this in mind, stand firm and be on guard with the power of prayer.

What God Says

> **Ephesians 6:10**
> "Finally, my brethren, be strong in the Lord, and in the power of his might"

✎ Express yourself * notes*

_____
_____
_____
_____

Your daily affirmation!
Calmness is the cradle of power." —J.G. Holland

Prayer

Lord, I thank you for being an amazing God, for being my comforter and my friend to the end, for being my counselor when I need guidance, and for being the autopilot to my once confused life.

I'm grateful to you for helping me to be more patient, for helping me to find the boldness to forgive those that hurt me, for helping me to know and understand my worth, and for availing me the spiritual sensitivity to be ready when it's time to fight.

I am forever grateful that I can call you my father.

This, I pray in your son, Jesus' name,

Amen.

THE BEGINNING OF MY WINNINGS

Life looks different when you are winning. No one likes to lose, no matter what. We detest the feeling of being 'the loser' and of all the things we fear, "You Lose" is among the top five. Athletes, singers, dancers, actors, even lawyers, irrespective of the opponent, we never want to be the one who lost.

Well, relax! Because, in this case, you WON! So, sit back and enjoy the fruits of your victory. You are a winner with God, through his mercy and grace. As the apostle Paul encouraged Timothy, while in prison, keep "fighting the good fight of the faith" (2Tim 4:1-8) and your continuous victory is sure. The urgency of finding love, from a place of pain, is over. Jesus has mended your grief and traumatic trails.

I challenge you today to accept Christ in your life and as soon as you feel His presence, seize him and keep holding on to him through it all, no matter what, never let go of your grasp.

As you grow in intimacy with Him, he'll become your lover and your friend, and in no time, you'll feel him like a current vibrating through – your hands, feet, body, heart, spirit, and soul. Choose to spend time to know Jesus. He's waiting for you to come to him, so that you can win together.

What God Says

1 Corinthians 9:24

"Do you not know that those who run in a race all run, but only one receives the prize? Run in such a way that you may win".

Express yourself * notes*

_____
_____
_____
_____

Your daily affirmation!

"If you don't see yourself as a winner, then you cannot perform as a winner".

Prayer

Lord, you have heard my loud voice from your throne crying for help. Forgive me for rejecting you, blaming you for my problems, for my attacks, and for my failures. I understand now that you were there all along.

O' God, you are so merciful and gracious that you've been waiting for me after all these years, but I have allowed my stubbornness to hinder my salvation.

I thank you for showing me my value, for helping to recognize the vision you have for my life, and for giving me the victory over my ordeals.

Hearing your voice through it all has humbled me in my faith and I bow in awe of your grace.

Lord, please continue to grant me the knowledge and understanding of your will.

I have never been free in my life, but now I can say that I have the VICTORY!

This, I pray in your son, Jesus' name,

Amen.

PRAYER FOR THE PREY
Poem by Erica Capri

It started on that day when those old hands that were supposed to protect me saw me as a buffet, and that is when, O God, I became a prey.

I can't explain with words how I felt, but for sure, I could feel my heart melt.

Why me? Why the one you say is your beloved?

The prayers for the prey, don't let it go away.

It was hard getting through this dark pain; I struggle morning, evening, and nights from going insane.

Yes, I went astray, even thinking about becoming gay.

I knew deep down that there is some faith, but how do I find it knowing I am being hunted as prey?

Can anyone see me? I want to be free and escape this

trauma that had me crying on my knees.

The prayers for the prey, yes I must obey,

Tell me, God, how can I move past being a sex slave?

Okay, I hear you, clearer than dew. Don't run to the many men they will take your kindness and vulnerability to screw.

Don't live in anger, rage, and hate because you don't want me to miss the twelve gates.

Don't settle for less, with all the stress, you're too beautiful and blessed.

Don't create bad habits of hopping all around to ease the pain.

The prayers for the prey, use it every day.

Today I am survivor, no more rival.

Today I am a priceless Queen, who's now washed and made clean.

Today I am a Winner, who was a sinner, but now a beginner.

Today I am just ME, what a way to be set FREE!

EXERCISE WORKBOOK

PUTTING PRAYERS TO ACTION

Burying the Past

Exercise #1

(The purpose of this exercise is to put your past behind you physically. When you bury something that brought you pain, it signifies that you are getting rid of your past or your ill habits. You are freeing yourself from all the negative energy in your life.)

EXERCISE #1

Take those names and bury them in something (ex. Ground, clothes, plants, grass, water etc.). Light three white candles. Then say these words ……..

> Dear God, I bury my past and the feelings of hurt I have over the people who have wronged me. I pray that you keep my mind, body, and soul free from now onward. My past and the people who have hurt me will no longer hinder me, because I know I have Jesus, your only begotten son, who died for me at Calvary. I let go of my past and now, I move on with my life without a shameful mask.

My Vision Board
Exercise #2

(This exercise will help you lay out your goals as a reminder to always stay on track.)

My Goals

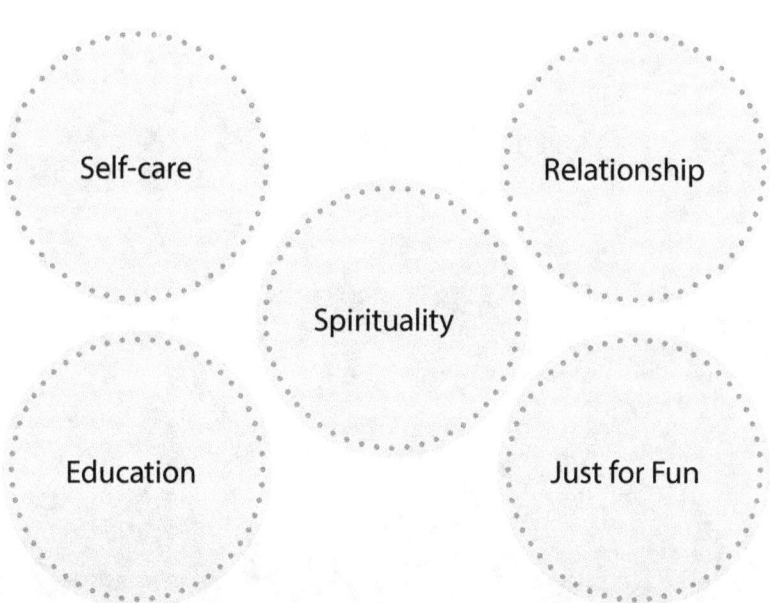

EXERCISE #2

Splitting your vision into categories helps to keep your goals in sight. When in sight, your goals become easily manageable. Once you're done completing this exercise, store it somewhere safe and secure, where you can access it daily.

Fast of Faith

Exercise #3

(This exercise is related to the Power of fasting and prayer. We hear God clearer when we take away earthly distractions and replace them with spiritual actions. There's an alarming atomic bomb that is released in the spiritual realm when we fast. It destroys every evil and every stronghold, and it opens the doors for more outpouring of the spirit into our lives.)

Acts 14:23

"Paul and Barnabas appointed elders for them in each church and, with prayer and fasting, committed them to the Lord, in whom they had put their trust."

EXERCISE #3

What is Fasting?

Fasting is when you are giving up earthly things of pleasure to dedicate time in God's presence – just you and Him, no distractions. You can essentially avoid food, social media, TV, etc. Fasting is accompanied by prayers, worship, and the study of the word.

What Does Fasting Do To Me?

1. Fasting can help us hear God clearer.

2. Fasting can open our spiritual eyes.

3. Fasting can strengthen our relationship with God.

4. Fasting helps build our prayer life.

5. Fasting helps build our faith in God.

Identify areas of pleasure and create a temporal restraint during your time of fasting for 3 days.

What to fast from • Food (the most common)

- Social Media
- TV/Movie (Sitcoms, shows, etc.)
- Secular Music

Day 1 – Fast against the Warfare waged by the enemy

*Pray every three hours *

Scriptures to read;

1. Psalms 44:5
2. Daniel 11:32
3. 2 Sam 22:3-4
4. Luke 10:9
5. 2 Corinthians 10:3-4
6. 1 Peter 5-:8-9
7. Colossians 2:15

Day 2 – Fast for Repentance & Guidance

*Pray every three hours *

Scriptures to read;

Repentance

1. Daniel 9:3-5

Guidance

2. Psalms 25:4-5
3. James 1-5-6
4. Psalms 5:8
5. Psalms 31:3

Day 3 – Fast for Strength

Pray every three hours

Scriptures to read;

1. Matt 17:20-21
2. Ezra 8:23

AUTHOR

"Erica T Capri"

ABOUT THE ATHOR

Erica T Capri is the author behind A Thin Line Trilogy Series. She is a stylist, film producer, entrepreneur, and playwright. Her work as playwright has become popular over the years with her production performing at Colleges and theatre stages. She's the rock star mother of two young children and COO of Gemlight Publishing LLC. Erica wrote over twenty pieces in the combination of stage plays, screenplays, children fiction, and novels. She has no plans to stop writing and hard at work on her book and film releases.

Follow the Author:

Facebook: Author Erica T Sherrill

Linkedin: Erica T Sherrill

Website: www.ericacapri.com

Email: ericasherrill77@gmail.com

OTHER TITLES BY THE AUTHOR

To Purchase more books visit:

www.gemlightpublishing.com/shop

Upcoming Title;

"How to Invest To Be Bless" (Self-help)

"No Trouble Today" (Children's Fiction)

Interested in joining our Gemlight Publishing family?
Visit our website for more details!

www.gemlightpublishing.com

Follow Us on Social Media ;

Facebook, Instagram, LinkedIn, & Twitter

Gemlight Publishing LLC Company
Attn: Erica T Sherrill /Publisher

gemlightpublishingllc@gmail.com
49 Hardy Court, Suite 385
Gulfport, MS 39507
833-436-5483 /Office

Thank you for your support.

Best wishes,

Erica T Capri

www.ingramcontent.com/pod-product-compliance
Lightning Source LLC
Chambersburg PA
CBHW052118070526
44584CB00017B/2542